THE BACKGROUND CHECK ADVANTAGE

"Making Informed Hiring Decisions"

Mr. A P Powale

AUTHOR'S MESSAGE

"The Background Check Advantage" is best suited for employers, HR professionals, and business owners looking to enhance their hiring practices and ensure a secure workforce. This comprehensive guide, authored by Mr. A P Powale, draws from his extensive experience in customer service, retail management, brand protection, and background screening to provide valuable insights and best practices. Whether you run a small business or a large corporation, this book equips you with the knowledge to conduct effective background checks, mitigate risks, and make informed hiring decisions. Additionally, individuals seeking to understand the importance of background screening in various industries will find this book valuable and informative.

Thank you to all the readers for choosing to explore "The Background Check Advantage." Your interest and engagement with the book are truly appreciated. I hope the insights shared within its pages empower you to make informed decisions, create secure environments, and drive success in your endeavors. Happy reading!

CONTENTS

CHAPTER 1: THE IMPORTANCE OF INFORMED HIRING

In today's competitive job market, finding the right talent for your organization is crucial for success. Making informed hiring decisions is not only about selecting candidates with the necessary skills and qualifications but also about ensuring that they align with your company's values and culture. This chapter explores the significance of background checks in the hiring process, shedding light on the potential consequences of overlooking this critical step.

The Cost of Bad Hires:

Hiring the wrong person can have far-reaching implications for your business. The financial costs of a bad hire extend beyond the recruitment process. When an unsuitable candidate is brought on board, they may not perform at the expected level, leading to lost productivity and additional training expenses. Moreover, the time invested in onboarding and integrating a new employee can go to waste, impacting the efficiency of your team.

Beyond the financial aspects, bad hires can also harm employee morale. When team members have to compensate for the shortcomings of an unfit colleague, it can lead to dissatisfaction and decreased engagement among your workforce. In severe cases, a bad hire may even cause internal conflicts or damage team dynamics.

Why Background Checks Matter:

Background checks are an invaluable tool for employers to assess the suitability of candidates before extending an offer of employment. By conducting these checks, you gain access to information that may not be evident from an applicant's resume or interview performance. It provides an opportunity to validate the accuracy of the information provided and identify any discrepancies or red flags.

Verifying Employment History: Background checks help ensure that the candidate's work experience matches what they have listed on their resume. This verification ensures that you are hiring someone with the relevant experience and skills required for the role.

Uncovering Criminal History: Criminal background checks are essential for positions that involve handling sensitive information, financial transactions, or dealing with vulnerable populations. Knowing about any past criminal history can help protect your company, customers, and employees.

Evaluating Educational Background: Educational verification ensures that the candidate possesses the necessary academic qualifications for the job. This is particularly crucial for roles that require specific degrees or certifications.

Making Smarter Hiring Decisions:

Background checks provide valuable insights that allow you to make more informed and objective hiring decisions. By having a comprehensive understanding of a candidate's past, you can assess their suitability for the position and your organization. These checks also enable you to identify candidates with a history of reliability and integrity, increasing the likelihood of a successful hire.

By investing in background screening, you demonstrate a commitment to due diligence and risk mitigation. It showcases your dedication to creating a safe and productive work environment for all employees. Moreover, conducting background checks consistently across all candidates ensures a fair and equitable hiring process, fostering a positive employer brand.

Conclusion:

The advantages of background checks in the hiring process

cannot be overstated. They protect your organization from potential risks associated with bad hires, while also supporting a more robust and effective hiring strategy. In the following chapters, we will delve deeper into the various types of background checks available, the legal implications and compliance considerations, and how to design an effective background screening policy that aligns with your company's needs and values.

CHAPTER 2: TYPES OF BACKGROUND CHECKS

In Chapter 1, we explored the significance of background checks in making informed hiring decisions. In this chapter, we'll look at the many types of background checks accessible to employers to examine an individual's past and character before making important choices such as hiring decisions. Here are several forms of background checks and their distinct functions in examining various aspects of a candidate's past, allowing you to gain a comprehensive understanding of their suitability for the job and your business.

Criminal Background Check:

Criminal history screening is one of the most critical aspects of background checks, especially for positions involving security, finance, healthcare, childcare, or any other sensitive roles. This type of screening helps identify any past criminal convictions or pending charges that could potentially impact the candidate's ability to perform the job responsibly and safely. It is essential to comply with local, state, and federal laws governing the use of criminal records in hiring decisions, such as the Fair Credit Reporting Act (FCRA).

Criminal history: This includes checking for any past convictions, arrests, or pending charges.

Sex offender registry: Verifies if the individual is listed as a registered sex offender.

Warrants: Determines if there are any outstanding warrants for the individual's arrest.

Identity Verification:

Social Security Number (SSN) verification: Ensures the SSN provided is valid and belongs to the individual.

Address history: Verifies past addresses to establish a consistent identity.

Driving Record Check:

Traffic violations: Identifies any speeding tickets, DUIs, or other driving offenses.

License status: Confirms the validity of the individual's driver's license.

Credit History Check:

Credit score: Assesses the individual's creditworthiness and financial responsibility.

Payment history: Reveals any late payments, defaults, or bankruptcies.

Outstanding debts: Provides information on outstanding loans or financial obligations.

Employment Verification:

This type of check provides valuable insights into the candidate's professional track record and helps verify the accuracy of the information provided on their resume.

Previous employment: Confirms the individual's work history, job titles, and dates of employment.

Job performance: This may include references or feedback from previous employers.

Eligibility for rehire: Ascertains if the individual is eligible to be rehired by previous employers.

Job responsibilities: Validates the roles and responsibilities held in previous positions.

Education Verification:

This verification process may require contacting universities or using third-party verification services.

Educational qualifications: Confirms the degrees, diplomas, or certifications claimed by the individual.

Educational institutions: Validate dates of attendance and graduation from educational institutions.

Reference Check:

This check is to gain insights into employees' character, work ethic, and overall suitability for the position.

Character references: Collects opinions from personal or professional references about the individual's behavior and abilities.

Professional references: Gather feedback from former colleagues or supervisors about the individual's work performance.

Social Media and Online Presence Check:

Scans social media platforms and online presence: Assesses the individual's public online behavior, posts, and content.

Drug and Health Screening:

Drug testing in background checks is a vital component of the employment process, serving as a proactive measure to maintain a safe and drug-free workplace. It is critical in certain industries and professional responsibilities where employee sobriety impacts safety, security, and job effectiveness. Positions in transportation, healthcare, law enforcement, heavy machinery operation, and other safety-sensitive fields should all undergo drug testing. Employers can confidently pick applicants who satisfy the essential requirements of sobriety by introducing drug testing into background checks, minimizing risks and ensuring a secure work environment for both employees and customers.

Conclusion:

Each type of background check serves a specific purpose in the hiring process, collectively allowing employers to assess a candidate's criminal history, work experience, educational qualifications, and character. By conducting these checks diligently and in compliance with relevant laws, you can build a reliable and trustworthy workforce, mitigating potential risks associated with making uninformed hiring decisions. In the next chapter, we will explore the legal regulations and compliance considerations that employers must be aware of when conducting background checks.

CHAPTER 3: COMPLYING WITH LEGAL REGULATIONS

In Chapter 2, we explored the different types of background checks available to employers. In this chapter, we will delve into the critical aspect of complying with legal regulations when conducting background checks. The hiring process must align with various federal, state, and local laws to ensure fairness, transparency, and protection of applicants' rights. Understanding and adhering to these regulations is essential to avoid legal pitfalls and potential lawsuits.

Understanding Employment Laws:
Employment laws are designed to protect both job applicants and employees from discrimination, privacy invasion, and other unfair practices. Some of the key federal laws that employers need to be aware of in the context of background checks include:

Fair Credit Reporting Act (FCRA):
The FCRA governs the acquisition, dissemination, and use of consumer information, including background checks. Employers must obtain written consent from candidates before conducting a background check through a Consumer Reporting Agency (CRA). If adverse action is taken based on the background check results, candidates must be provided with a pre-adverse action notice, a copy of their consumer report, and a summary of rights. After taking adverse action, employers must also provide an adverse action notice.

Title VII of the Civil Rights Act:
Title VII prohibits discrimination based on race, color, religion,

sex, or national origin in the hiring process. Background checks must be applied uniformly to all candidates and should not disproportionately impact protected groups.

Americans with Disabilities Act (ADA):
The ADA prohibits discrimination against individuals with disabilities and places limitations on the types of questions employers can ask about an applicant's medical history.

Fair Hiring Practices and "Ban the Box" Legislation:

"Ban the Box" is a movement that aims to remove the checkbox on job applications asking candidates about their criminal history. Several states and local jurisdictions have adopted "Ban the Box" legislation to ensure that candidates are not automatically disqualified based on their criminal record, allowing them a fair chance to be evaluated based on their qualifications.

Reviewing State and Local Laws: "Ban the Box" laws can vary significantly by jurisdiction, so employers need to review the specific regulations in their location.

Timing of Criminal History Inquiries: Ensure that inquiries about an applicant's criminal history are deferred until later stages of the hiring process or after a conditional job offer has been made.

The Role of EEOC in Background Screening:

The Equal Employment Opportunity Commission (EEOC) is responsible for enforcing federal laws that prohibit employment discrimination. Employers should be mindful of the EEOC's guidance on using criminal history information in hiring decisions.

Individualized Assessment: When considering a candidate's criminal history, employers should conduct an individualized assessment, taking into account the nature and gravity of the offense, the time elapsed since the conviction, and the relevance to the job.

Business Necessity: Employers should be able to demonstrate a legitimate business necessity for excluding candidates with certain criminal records from specific positions.

Conclusion:

Compliance with legal regulations is a critical aspect of the background screening process. By adhering to the Fair Credit Reporting Act, Title VII, Americans with Disabilities Act, "Ban the Box" legislation, and EEOC guidance, employers can conduct background checks fairly and lawfully. In the next chapter, we will discuss how to design an effective background screening policy that aligns with legal requirements and best practices, promoting a trustworthy and successful hiring process.

CHAPTER 4: DESIGNING AN EFFECTIVE BACKGROUND SCREENING POLICY

In Chapter 3, we explored the importance of complying with legal regulations when conducting background checks. In this chapter, we will focus on designing a comprehensive and effective background screening policy that aligns with your organization's needs, values, and legal requirements. A well-designed policy ensures consistency, fairness, and transparency in the hiring process, enabling you to make informed and reliable hiring decisions.

Tailoring Background Checks to Job Roles:

Different positions within your organization may require varying levels of background screening. Tailoring background checks to each job role helps ensure that you are conducting appropriate and relevant screenings.

Risk Level: Assess the risk associated with each job role. Positions that involve handling sensitive information, financial responsibilities, or working with vulnerable populations may require more extensive background checks.

Legal Requirements: Ensure that the background checks conducted for each job role comply with relevant federal, state, and local laws.

Developing a Transparent and Consistent Screening Process

A transparent and consistent screening process is essential for building trust with candidates and avoiding potential legal issues.

Communicate your background screening policy to applicants and follow the same process for all candidates to avoid any appearance of bias or discrimination.

Written Policy: Have a written background screening policy that outlines the types of checks conducted, the timing of the checks, and the procedures for obtaining candidate consent.

Clear Communication: Inform candidates about the background screening process early in the hiring process, ideally before initiating any checks. Provide them with information about their rights under the Fair Credit Reporting Act (FCRA) and other applicable laws.

Securing Applicant Consent: Best Practices for Disclosure and Authorization

Before conducting any background checks, employers must obtain written consent from candidates. The consent should be clear, separate from other application materials, and comply with the requirements outlined in the Fair Credit Reporting Act (FCRA).

Standalone Disclosure: The disclosure form should be a separate document that clearly and conspicuously informs the candidate that a background check will be conducted.

Authorization Form: The candidate should sign an authorization form giving the employer permission to conduct the background checks.

Leveraging Technology for Background Screening

Technology can streamline the background screening process and improve its efficiency. Many employers use applicant tracking systems (ATS) to manage the hiring workflow, including background checks.

Integrating Background Checks: Integrate background checks seamlessly into your ATS to manage candidate information and streamline the screening process.

Data Security: Ensure that any third-party screening providers you work with prioritize data security and confidentiality.

Adverse Action and FCRA Compliance:

In some cases, the information uncovered in a background check may lead to adverse actions, such as withdrawing a job offer or taking other negative employment actions. It is crucial to follow the proper procedures outlined in the Fair Credit Reporting Act (FCRA) to remain compliant.

Pre-Adverse Action Notice: Before taking adverse action, provide the candidate with a pre-adverse action notice that includes a copy of their consumer report and a summary of rights.

Adverse Action Notice: After taking adverse action, provide the candidate with an adverse action notice, informing them of the decision and their rights.

Conclusion:

Designing an effective background screening policy is essential for maintaining a reliable, fair, and legally compliant hiring process. By tailoring background checks to job roles, ensuring transparency and consistency, securing applicant consent, leveraging technology, and adhering to adverse action and FCRA compliance, you can create a background screening process that supports informed hiring decisions and reinforces your commitment to a trustworthy workforce. In the next chapter, we will explore how to spot red flags and mitigate risks during the background screening process.

CHAPTER 5: SPOTTING RED FLAGS AND MITIGATING RISKS

I n Chapter 4, we discussed designing an effective background screening policy to ensure a reliable and legally compliant hiring process. In this chapter, we will focus on the crucial task of spotting red flags during background checks and implementing strategies to mitigate potential risks associated with certain findings.

Identifying Dishonesty and Inconsistencies in Resumes

Background checks are valuable tools for verifying the information provided by candidates on their resumes. While most candidates are honest, some may exaggerate their qualifications or experience to appear more suitable for the job. It is essential to spot any discrepancies or signs of dishonesty during the screening process.

Cross-Checking Employment History: Verify the dates of employment, job titles, and responsibilities with previous employers to ensure accuracy.

Confirming Educational Background: Validate academic degrees and certifications to ensure they are legitimate and relevant to the job.

Dealing with Gaps in Employment History

Gaps in employment history can be concerning for employers, as they may indicate periods of unemployment or unaccounted activities. While some gaps are legitimate, others may require further investigation to understand the reasons behind them.

Conducting Interviews: Ask candidates about any employment gaps to understand the reasons behind them. Sometimes, gaps are due to personal reasons such as family responsibilities or educational pursuits.

Assessing Work Readiness: Consider the candidate's overall qualifications, experience, and skills to determine their readiness for the job, irrespective of any employment gaps.

Addressing Criminal Records: Rehabilitation and Second Chances

Discovering a candidate's criminal history can be challenging for employers. However, it is essential to remember that individuals can reform and rehabilitate after past mistakes. Deciding how to handle criminal records requires a careful and balanced approach.

Individualized Assessment: Consider the nature of the offense, its relevance to the job, the time that has elapsed since the conviction, and evidence of rehabilitation.

Compliance with EEOC Guidance: Follow the Equal Employment Opportunity Commission's (EEOC) guidance to avoid potential discrimination based on criminal history.

Evaluating Financial History for Relevant Positions

For positions involving financial responsibilities or access to sensitive financial data, evaluating a candidate's financial history can be crucial. However, it's essential to balance the need for financial scrutiny with the applicant's rights and privacy.

Relevance to the Position: Only conduct financial history checks for positions where it is directly relevant, such as roles involving financial transactions or handling company funds.

Compliance with FCRA: Ensure compliance with the Fair Credit Reporting Act (FCRA) and any state-specific regulations governing the use of credit reports in employment decisions.

Utilizing Professional Reference Checks

Professional reference checks provide valuable insights into a candidate's work ethic, performance, and interpersonal skills. Leveraging these references can help you make more informed hiring decisions.

Engaging Former Supervisors: Prioritize speaking with individuals who directly supervised the candidate to gain a comprehensive understanding of their work performance.

Asking Relevant Questions: Prepare a list of specific questions to ask references to gather meaningful and relevant feedback about the candidate.

Conclusion

Spotting red flags and mitigating risks during the background screening process is vital for making informed and responsible hiring decisions. By identifying dishonesty, addressing employment gaps, assessing criminal records fairly, evaluating financial history cautiously, and utilizing professional reference checks, employers can build a strong and reliable workforce. In the next chapter, we will explore other considerations beyond background checks, such as skills assessments, cultural fit evaluation, and behavioral interviews, to further refine the hiring process and select the best candidates for your organization.

CHAPTER 6: BEYOND BACKGROUND CHECKS: OTHER HIRING CONSIDERATIONS

I n Chapter 5, we discussed the importance of spotting red flags and mitigating risks during the background screening process. In this chapter, we will explore additional hiring considerations beyond background checks. These considerations focus on evaluating a candidate's skills, cultural fit, and behavioral traits to further refine the hiring process and select the best candidates for your organization.

Assessing Skills and Competencies

While background checks provide valuable information about a candidate's past experiences, assessing their skills and competencies is essential to determine their ability to perform the job successfully. Skill assessments can be used to objectively measure a candidate's proficiency in specific areas.

Job-Related Assessments: Tailor skill assessments to align with the specific requirements of the job. For example, if the role requires proficiency in a particular software program, conduct a hands-on assessment to evaluate the candidate's proficiency.

Consistency and Fairness: Ensure that skill assessments are administered consistently to all candidates for the same position to avoid bias.

Cultural Fit and Team Dynamics

Cultural fit is a crucial factor in ensuring long-term success and satisfaction for both the candidate and the organization. Assessing cultural fit involves evaluating how well a candidate's values, work style, and personality align with the company's culture and the existing team dynamics.

Define Your Company Culture: Clearly define your organization's values, mission, and work culture to identify the traits and qualities you seek in potential hires.

Behavioral Interviewing: Conduct behavioral interviews to gain insights into how candidates have handled past situations and how they would respond to scenarios relevant to your company's culture.

Behavioral Interviews: Revealing Traits and Predicting Performance

Behavioral interviews are designed to explore a candidate's past behavior and how they handled specific situations. These interviews provide valuable information about a candidate's problem-solving abilities, communication skills, and emotional intelligence.

Structured Interview Questions: Prepare a set of standardized behavioral interview questions to ensure consistency and fairness across all candidates.

STAR Method: Use the STAR method (Situation, Task, Action, Result) to guide candidates in providing detailed responses about their past experiences and accomplishments.

Balancing Skills, Cultural Fit, and Background Screening

While each aspect of the hiring process offers valuable insights, it is crucial to strike a balance between skills, cultural fit, and background screening. An ideal candidate possesses not only the necessary skills and experience but also fits well within the company culture.

Weighted Criteria: Assign appropriate weightage to each aspect of the hiring process based on the job's requirements and the organization's values.

Collaborative Decision-Making: Involve multiple stakeholders, such as hiring managers and team members, in the decision-making process to gain diverse perspectives.

Second Interviews and Assessment Center Activities

For top candidates, conducting second interviews or assessment center activities can provide a deeper understanding of their abilities, work style, and potential contributions to the organization.

Role-Play Exercises: Create scenarios that simulate real workplace situations to observe how candidates handle challenges and interact with others.

Team Collaboration: Encourage candidates to collaborate with existing team members during assessment center activities to assess how they fit within the team.

Conclusion

Beyond background checks, evaluating skills, cultural fit, and behavioral traits are crucial steps in making successful and sustainable hiring decisions. By assessing skills and competencies, considering cultural fit and team dynamics, conducting behavioral interviews, balancing hiring considerations, and incorporating second interviews or assessment center activities, employers can refine their hiring process and select candidates who not only have the right qualifications but also contribute positively to the organization's success. In the next chapter, we will explore the importance of engaging a reliable background screening provider and communicating screening results with candidates.

CHAPTER 7: ENGAGING A RELIABLE BACKGROUND SCREENING PROVIDER

In Chapter 6, we explored various hiring considerations beyond background checks, such as assessing skills, cultural fit, and behavioral traits. In this chapter, we will focus on the importance of engaging a reliable background screening provider. Partnering with a reputable screening provider ensures accurate, compliant, and efficient background checks, enabling employers to make well-informed hiring decisions.

The Role of a Background Screening Provider

A background screening provider plays a critical role in the hiring process. They are experts in conducting thorough background checks, verifying candidate information, and providing valuable insights that help employers assess a candidate's suitability for the job.

Expertise and Experience: Choose a provider with a proven track record and extensive experience in the background screening industry.

Compliance Knowledge: Ensure the provider is well-versed in relevant federal, state, and local laws governing background checks to avoid legal issues.

Comprehensive Background Checks Offered

Different positions require different types of background checks. A reliable screening provider should offer a comprehensive range of screening services tailored to your organization's needs.

Criminal History Screening: Ensure the provider conducts criminal history checks at the county, state, and federal levels to identify potential red flags.

Employment Verification: Verify past employment history and job responsibilities to confirm a candidate's work experience.

Educational Background Verification: Validate academic degrees, certifications, and credentials to ensure accuracy.

Turnaround Time and Efficiency

Time is of the essence in the hiring process. A reliable background screening provider should deliver timely and efficient results, allowing you to make hiring decisions promptly.

Average Processing Time: Inquire about the provider's average turnaround time for different types of background checks.

System Integration: Assess whether the provider's services can be integrated into your applicant tracking system (ATS) for a seamless hiring process.

Data Security and Privacy

Handling sensitive candidate information requires the utmost care and security. A reputable screening provider should have robust data security measures in place to protect applicant privacy.

Compliance with Industry Standards: Verify that the provider adheres to industry standards for data security and privacy, such as ISO 27001 certification.

Confidentiality Measures: Assess the provider's policies on data retention and access to ensure confidential candidate information is safeguarded.

Transparent Pricing and Support

Engaging a background screening provider involves financial considerations. It is essential to understand the provider's pricing structure and the level of support they offer throughout the screening process.

Pricing Structure: Request a clear breakdown of costs for different types of background checks and any additional services.

Customer Support: Evaluate the provider's customer support capabilities and responsiveness to address any questions or concerns promptly.

Conclusion

Engaging a reliable background screening provider is essential for obtaining accurate, compliant, and timely background check results. By selecting a provider with expertise, comprehensive screening services, efficient turnaround times, robust data security measures, transparent pricing, and excellent customer support, employers can confidently make informed hiring decisions. In the next chapter, we will explore the crucial aspect of communicating background screening results with candidates and the steps to take when adverse action is required based on the findings.

CHAPTER 8: COMMUNICATING BACKGROUND SCREENING RESULTS WITH CANDIDATES

I n Chapter 7, we discussed the importance of engaging a reliable background screening provider. In this chapter, we will focus on the crucial aspect of communicating background screening results with candidates. Effectively communicating the findings to candidates and following appropriate procedures, including adverse action, when necessary, ensures fairness, transparency, and compliance throughout the hiring process.

The Importance of Clear and Timely Communication
Clear and timely communication with candidates about background screening results is essential to maintain a positive candidate experience and uphold your organization's reputation. Candidates have the right to know the outcome of their background checks and understand how the results may impact their candidacy.

Timely Disclosure: Inform candidates promptly about the background screening process and any potential delays in obtaining results.

Transparency: Be transparent about the information revealed in the background check and how it aligns with the job requirements and company policies.

Providing Pre-Adverse Action Notice

When background check results raise concerns that may lead to adverse action, such as withdrawing a job offer or denying employment, it is crucial to provide candidates with a pre-adverse action notice.

Explanation of Results: Clearly explain the specific findings that led to the consideration of adverse action.

Copy of Consumer Report: Provide a copy of the consumer report obtained from the background screening provider.

Summary of Rights: Include a summary of the candidate's rights under the Fair Credit Reporting Act (FCRA).

Allowing Candidates to Dispute Inaccurate Information

The FCRA grants candidates the right to dispute inaccurate information in their consumer reports. If a candidate disputes the results of their background check, the employer must conduct a reasonable investigation to verify the accuracy of the information.

Timely Response: Respond promptly to candidate disputes and initiate a reasonable investigation within the required timeframe under the FCRA.

Collaboration with the Screening Provider: Work closely with the background screening provider to verify the accuracy of the disputed information.

Taking Adverse Action and Providing Adverse Action Notice

In cases where adverse action is taken based on background check results, employers must provide candidates with an adverse action notice. This notice informs candidates of the decision and their rights, allowing them to address any inaccuracies or mitigating factors.

Adverse Decision: Clearly state the decision to take adverse action based on the background check results.

Contact Information: Provide contact information for the background screening provider so candidates can inquire about the results or dispute inaccuracies.

Complying with Ban the Box Legislation

If your jurisdiction has "Ban the Box" legislation, which restricts when and how employers can inquire about a candidate's criminal history, ensure compliance with the applicable laws.

Timing of Criminal History Inquiry: Inquire about a candidate's criminal history at a lawful stage of the hiring process, as per local legislation.

Individualized Assessment: Conduct an individualized assessment of a candidate's criminal history, considering the nature of the offense and its relevance to the job.

Conclusion:

Communicating background screening results with candidates is a critical part of the hiring process. By providing timely and transparent communication, offering pre-adverse action and adverse action notices, allowing candidates to dispute inaccurate information, and complying with Ban the Box legislation where applicable, employers can maintain a fair and compliant hiring process. In the next chapter, we will discuss the importance of periodic screening for existing employees to ensure ongoing trust and safety within the organization.

CHAPTER 9: PERIODIC SCREENING FOR EXISTING EMPLOYEES

I n Chapter 8, we explored the importance of communicating background screening results with candidates and adhering to adverse action procedures. In this chapter, we will focus on the significance of conducting periodic background screenings for existing employees. Periodic screening helps employers ensure the ongoing trustworthiness, safety, and security of their workforce, especially for roles that involve access to sensitive information or regular interaction with vulnerable populations.

The Importance of Ongoing Employee Screening

Background screening is not a one-time event but an ongoing process that supports a safe and secure work environment. Periodic screening for existing employees allows employers to identify any new red flags or changes in their backgrounds that may impact their suitability for their current roles.

Employee Trust and Safety: Periodic screening helps maintain the trust of customers, clients, and colleagues by continuously ensuring the integrity of the workforce.

Mitigating Risk: By identifying potential issues proactively, employers can mitigate risks associated with employee misconduct or lapses in qualifications.

Types of Periodic Screening

The types of periodic screening conducted may vary depending on the nature of the job, industry regulations, and company policies. Common types of periodic screening include criminal background checks, credit checks (where applicable and permissible by law), and verification of licenses and certifications.

Criminal Background Checks: Conducting regular criminal history screenings helps employers stay informed about any new criminal convictions that may impact an employee's suitability for their position.

Credit Checks: For roles that involve financial responsibilities, credit checks may be relevant to assess an employee's financial stability and integrity.

Compliance with Employment Laws

When conducting periodic screenings, it is essential to remain compliant with relevant employment laws, such as the Fair Credit Reporting Act (FCRA) and any state-specific regulations.

Obtain Consent: Just as with initial background checks, employers must obtain written consent from employees before conducting periodic screenings.

Adhere to State and Local Regulations: Be aware of any state or local laws that may impact the frequency and scope of periodic screenings.

Balancing Privacy and Security:

While periodic screening is essential for maintaining a safe work environment, it is crucial to balance employee privacy with the need for security and risk management.

Communicate Policies: Ensure that employees are aware of the company's policy regarding periodic screenings and how the results will be used.

Limit Scope to Job Relevance: Focus on screening information that is directly relevant to the employee's job responsibilities.

Addressing Adverse Findings in Ongoing Screening:

In some cases, periodic screenings may uncover new information that raises concerns about an employee's continued suitability for their role. It is essential to address adverse findings promptly and fairly.

Individualized Assessment: Conduct an individualized assessment of the adverse findings and consider relevant factors before taking any adverse action.

Employee Communication: Communicate with the employee openly and transparently about the results and any potential consequences.

Conclusion:

Periodic screening for existing employees is a crucial practice to ensure ongoing trust, safety, and security within the organization. By conducting regular screenings, remaining compliant with employment laws, balancing privacy and security, and addressing adverse findings fairly, employers can maintain a reliable and trustworthy workforce. In the final chapter, we will summarize the key takeaways and reinforce the importance of background screening in making informed hiring decisions and building a successful organization.

CHAPTER 10:
CONCLUSION - THE
BACKGROUND CHECK
ADVANTAGE

T hroughout this book, we have explored the significance of background screening in the hiring process and maintaining a safe and trustworthy workforce. The Background Check Advantage lies in making informed hiring decisions, mitigating risks, and upholding fairness and compliance in the hiring process. In this concluding chapter, we will summarize the key takeaways and reinforce the importance of background screening in building a successful and reliable organization.

The Key Benefits of Background Screening

Background screening offers numerous benefits to employers, including:

Risk Mitigation: Conducting thorough background checks helps identify red flags and potential risks associated with candidates, reducing the likelihood of making hiring decisions that could harm the organization.

Enhanced Hiring Decisions: By verifying qualifications, work history, and character, background checks enable employers to make informed and objective hiring decisions, leading to a more robust and more competent workforce.

Legal Compliance: Adhering to federal, state, and local employment laws, such as the Fair Credit Reporting Act (FCRA) and "Ban the Box" legislation, ensures a fair and legally compliant hiring process.

Trust and Reputation: Prioritizing background screening instills trust among customers, clients, and stakeholders, enhancing the organization's reputation as a responsible and reliable employer.

Designing an Effective Background Screening Policy

Creating a comprehensive and effective background screening policy involves:

Tailoring Checks to Job Roles: Customize background checks based on the specific requirements of each position within the organization.

Transparent and Consistent Process: Ensure a transparent and consistent screening process, providing candidates with clear communication about the screening process and their rights.

Secure Applicant Consent: Obtain written consent from candidates before initiating background checks through a reputable background screening provider.

Spotting Red Flags and Mitigating Risks

Identifying red flags during background checks is crucial, along with strategies to mitigate risks:

Identifying Dishonesty: Cross-checking information on resumes and verifying employment and educational backgrounds helps identify dishonesty.

Addressing Employment Gaps: Conducting interviews and assessing overall qualifications assist in understanding the reasons behind employment gaps.

Beyond Background Checks: Other Hiring Considerations

Apart from background checks, considering skills, cultural fit, and behavioral traits during the hiring process adds valuable insights:

Assessing Skills and Competencies: Utilizing skill assessments helps evaluate candidates' abilities to perform job-specific tasks.

Cultural Fit and Team Dynamics: Evaluating cultural fit helps maintain a cohesive and harmonious work environment.

Behavioral Interviews: Conducting behavioral interviews reveals past behaviors and problem-solving abilities.

Engaging a Reliable Background Screening Provider

Partnering with a reputable background screening provider ensures accurate and compliant results:

Expertise and Experience: Selecting a provider with a strong track record and compliance knowledge ensures reliable results.

Comprehensive Background Checks: Choosing a provider that offers various screening services tailored to organizational needs ensures a thorough process.

Communicating Screening Results and Periodic Screening

Clear communication with candidates about screening results and conducting periodic screenings for existing employees is essential:

Timely and Transparent Communication: Keeping candidates informed about results maintains a positive candidate experience.

Periodic Screening: Conducting ongoing screenings ensures continued trust and safety within the organization.

Conclusion:

The Background Check Advantage empowers employers to make well-informed hiring decisions, protect their organization from risks, and build a trustworthy workforce. By designing an effective background screening policy, spotting red flags, considering other hiring aspects, engaging a reliable screening provider, communicating results effectively, and conducting periodic screenings, employers can create a strong foundation for success. Embracing background screening as an integral part of the hiring process reinforces a commitment to building a safe, competent, and reputable organization.

www.ingramcontent.com/pod-product-compliance
Lightning Source LLC
Chambersburg PA
CBHW072224290526
45794CB00007B/2875